MW00935896

Time Sheets

A Collection of Poems

Stephen R Wagner

Copyright © 2014 Stephen R Wagner

All rights reserved.

ISBN: 1494868091
ISBN-13: 978-1494868093

Dedication

I am indebted to my mother for the compilation and creation of this volume. It was she who gathered all of the collected poems here and assembled them from notes I had sent her over the years. And for that, I am tremendously grateful. Without her there would be no book.

I am also indebted to my wife, Susan, who has kept me alive and focused, throughout all the nonsense. Without her there would be no me.

Last, but not least, this book is dedicated to my two daughters, Sophie and Cecelia. For whom I will continue to strive to be a decent father. Without them there would be no joy.

Preface

For many years it has been my responsibility to ensure that all of my coworkers submit their time sheets on a regular and timely basis: a process that has always been an uphill battle. When I was younger, I fiercely chased down tardy submitters to the point that, too often, I found myself in pointless shouting matches, arguing about the merits of doing the work versus recording it.

I became more and more embattled until I finally came to the resolution to distance myself from the process altogether. I would individually hunt down the wayward Tuesday through Friday, but Monday would serve as a reprieve: a day on which I could simply send a poem to serve as a general reminder that such things as "time sheets" exist.

These poems, selfishly, were and are created entirely to appease my own need for them. And, of course, they don't really have anything to do with time sheets at all.

Monday, December 22, 2008

Having waded through the snow
At the door
And reached for the shovel
Under the eaves
I am reminded by the rake
Behind it
Of plans made to gather the leaves
And it is difficult to reconcile
That neither the leaves
Nor the time sheets
Will be properly gathered this season
If at all

Monday, December 29, 2008

As I was first startled
By the sudden disappearance
Of the fall leaves beneath the snow
It is even more startling
To see their reemergence now
And to see
So clearly
That they have not somehow
Raked themselves up
Nor properly covered
The time sheets
That curl
Unsubmitted
Among them

Monday, January 5, 2009

The old year slips away
So quickly
That the new year
Left in its place
Seems foreign and strange
Lost like a small child
Who's been left standing at the bus station
With time sheets sticking out of her pockets

Monday, January 12, 2009

Too cold
In the northernmost states
To drive or fly
Or think
Wet logs are wrapped in time sheets
To encourage them to burn

Tuesday, January 20, 2009

Due to the fact that it no longer seems to stop snowing
But rather, only pauses
And that cobblestone driveways
Have long since given up their navigability
With the accumulated slush and time sheets
Pressed beneath the tires
It was perhaps inevitable
That the mini mini-van
Would become lodged sideways along the banks
Only to be removed later
By the backhoe
Groaning in the dark
Pushing the ground
With its outstretched arms
Pulling its tethered charge
And itself
Upwards
Inch by inch
Towards the light
At the top of the drive

Monday, January 26, 2009

Arctic shelves heave and threaten to fall apart
Remaining moored only by sinews and chance
While the arctic weather itself
Has already broken free
From constraints of place
And roams wildly over the continents
Withering and seizing
Even the most basic elements
Of movement and transportation
Only then to relent
And then solidify again
Hammering the streets and trees
With frozen time sheets
As clear and as hard
As glass

Monday, February 2, 2009

At the end
Or, towards the end
Of winters that know no rest
Or peace
Private citizens become
Amateur engineers
Trying to calculate
Whether the swollen ice dams
Stuck to their roofs like lampreys
Will kill the host and
Force a structural collapse
Or, if, perhaps
They will dissipate
On their own
Rescinding the threats they have made
And release the tender shingles
From their grasp

Small brittle shingles
Which have been clinging
Tentatively
To nothing but the tar paper
And packed time sheets
Hidden beneath

Monday, February 9, 2009

With the snow globe
On the mantel
No longer being rabidly shaken
We find ourselves
In the midst
Of a single tepid weekend
With temperatures
Not yet warm
But rather, absent of the cold

A two day period
Capable of assuaging
The damages of a season
To see briefly
Yet clearly
The possibility of spring
The remnants of time sheets
Thawing on the bottom
Of the recycling bin
Curling their once frozen edges
Like leaves towards the sun

Monday, February 16, 2009

Still cold enough to frost windshields
In the mornings
Yet the quality and caliber of light
That somehow manages to get through
Increases daily
In a noticeable enough way
That the fish in the aquarium
Begin to change their eating patterns
Nipping at the bits of time sheets
That dissolve above them
Cognizant of the rise of spring

Monday, February 23, 2009

It is during the minor storms
Towards the end of the season
That one is better able to appreciate
The positives of the winter
There is something very satisfying
In the uniformity
Of a layer of snow
A clear and discernible thing
Somehow managing to cover
All that it has encountered
As if part of the rock strata
The thinnest of geological records
The shortest of eras
Hardly thicker than a layer of time sheets
Gone almost before it has arrived

Monday, March 9 2009

Standing in the early morning slush
It occurs to me that there is a certain wisdom
In being a late bloomer
For it is the first bulbs and buds
Of the spring
That are met with nothing but
Rain and ice
After having seen the sun for only a few hours

Better to lie still for a while
Underneath the surface
Beneath the packed down time sheets
Keeping company with the leaves and pebbles
For a while

Monday, March 16, 2009

Warm enough to stand outside
On a patch of clear ground
Surrounded now
Only by scattered and thinned crusts of snow
There are gritty remnants of time sheets here
Unsubmitted project time
Moves across the sky
Like clouds

Monday, March 23, 2009

As if proof
Of the resilience of all things
The flattened tires of the old bicycles
Dragged out of storage
On the third day of spring
Beneath skies that threaten rain
The tires hold the air that is pumped into them
And transform easily into rigid wheels
Capable of transporting all of the yet unknown
Loads of the season

Wrapped packages of time sheets
Wait on the lawn
To be placed into baskets
And ferried to their destinations

Monday, March 30, 2009

Peepers begin to call
From the trees
On either side of the creek-bed
The ground softens
And a warm fog rolls in
Obscuring the view through the trees
Such that individual lines
On the time sheets hung in the woods
Cannot be read
But rather, blur together
As if musical notes running over a page

Monday, April 6, 2009

Puttering around the yard
At the beginning of the season
With the weather still
On the cold side of neutral
Everything seems slightly off
Dirtier and more faded
Than it should
As if the whole yard needed a coat of paint

Time sheets peel from the sides of the garage
And sit inside in damp clumps
On the rafters

Monday, April 13, 2009

The sun and the wind
Compete for strength
As the children
Shuttle across the lawn
Diligently harvesting
The plastic eggs
Which hide
The carefully folded time sheets within

Monday, April 20, 2009

Weary of shredding
All of the old sensitivities
Five to seven sheets at a time
The old documentation
Is pulled from its windowed envelopes
And brought to the fire pit
Where it twists upwards
As red-rimmed gray ash
Caught below the mesh screen
Along with the remainder
Of last season's time sheets

Monday, April 27, 2009

In the abruptness of change
The snowblower is pushed
Still full of gas
Further back into the garage
Not to be maintained
Or addressed
Until the sun trails away to nothing
And sheaves of time sheets again fall from the sky
Blotting out the blue
With their white

Monday, May 4, 2009

Spring crawls out from the creek bed
Behind our house
And makes itself known
In the shape of a twisting garter snake
Under last year's time sheets
By the walk

And as a turtle
Almost stepped upon
At the foot of the deck
Small, round
And gray
Almost indistinct from the asphalt
But orange-bellied and wild underneath
With tiny legs
Swimming through the air

Monday, May 11, 2009

And, now, when we hear
The Canadian geese fly overhead
The tone of their calls seems chattier
And, to see them
Their formations seem smaller, more informal

It is not even always clear
As to which direction they are headed
It is nothing like
Before the winter
When they moved in rigid unison
Pointing with a seriousness of purpose
Away from the hard-packed time sheets
That stretched across the grounds of the North

Monday, May 18, 2009

Working on the upper deck
Of a two-story children's play set
Made up of eight hundred pounds
Of wood and fasteners
White petals fall from the overhanging branches
Which brush my shoulders
As I attach the fort's roof
To the upper railings
And I am struck by the profound relationship
Of civilization to trees
How intrinsic the wood is to everything
And how reliable it's been
Safe and malleable
Ready to be cut to pieces
Or chopped up and turned to mash
Pressed into service as
Foundations and braces
Or rolled out into
Meaningless
Time sheets

Monday, June 1, 2009

Having traveled to the beach
By my home
For the first time in more than a year
It occurs to me
That I had forgotten
How close I was to the ocean

How else could I not have come
More often
To watch the waves
Spin down into the sand
And drag the sediment
Covering all the time sheets
Back out to sea

Monday, June 8, 2009

The lawn is a mismatched array of heights
Towering knee-high seeded grasses
Shift to weedy mixes and eventually
Raw earth
Beneath the trees at the edges

It is the lawnmower
On its lowest setting
That equalizes the field
Bringing everything down

I have read that as the blade dulls
It no longer cuts
But, in fact, tears
I wonder if it is doing so now
As the nest-like flotsam
Drifts out from beneath it

I know without looking
That the wet green cores of the grass
Are pinned to the inside casing
Of the machine
The liquid green chlorophyll
Pasting the remains
Of grass and leaves and time sheets
To the metal

Tuesday, June 16, 2009

There was only one man in the goat pit
On that rainy day at the petting zoo
He had gone in
I'm told
At the request of others

He could be seen trying to shift
A baby
Up onto on his shoulder
While the surrounding goats
Stood on their hind legs around him and
Placed their hooves
On his stomach, back and legs
As perches
To better get at the swirling food
Jostled out of the conical
Time sheet wrapper

Monday, June 22, 2009

In that particular year
The transition from spring to summer
Went unnoticed
As there were no changes or differences
To speak of

The rain grew no warmer
And the sun
Not pressed by guilt or duty
Made no appearance
The date passed with no fanfare
In unobserved motion
Like the waters of an underground tributary
Seemingly inconsequential
One day listed after the next
An unbroken week
On an indifferent time sheet

Monday, July 6, 2009

When the clouds themselves
Finally became annoyed and left
The people rejoiced
With rockets and munitions
They targeted the very sky itself
As if in retaliation

Rows of tightly packed cardboard tubes
With colored time sheets
Pasted on their sides
Showed boastful descriptions
Of the weapons
To be deployed

Monday, July 13, 2009

Unexpected rains
Late in the morning
Caught the paperwork
Left out by the table
Cementing it into place

When it was peeled off
An impression remained
A partial row from a time sheet
Crisp at the center
Blurred to nothing
Along the edge

Monday, July 20, 2009

Unseasonal rains
Work to slowly transform the season
Into something else
That will only be identified in hindsight

Record rains
Seep to record depths
Activating dormant creatures
Such as mosquitoes and time sheets
And other strange things
Put into place years before
And then forgotten

Monday, July 27, 2009

In an era of small things
Effort must be made
To gather together
The giant lurching creatures
Of the past

At makeshift docks
Alongside the jetty
Where the river ends
The Tall Ships rock quietly

A tangle of rigging
Like a thousand crossed power lines
Anchored to thick masts
That have yet to be shaved down
Into countless time sheets

Monday, August 3, 2009

Coming towards the end of our supply
Of superworms
It occurred to me that I had done nothing
Other than feed them to the fish

We had started out
With dozens
And were now down to just a few
Three or four, perhaps, in each container
Crawling aimlessly
In the time sheet shavings
That kept them nourished

So I took a container into the yard
And released them
Onto the grass
Where I thought they would flounder
For an uncomfortably long time
Making me reconsider my actions
But they disappeared
In seconds
And I felt refreshed

Monday, August 10, 2009

With all the mysteries
Of the sky
There are still only
Four types of clouds
Which drift languorously across

As though the white-space on a time sheet
Had lifted off the page
On a whim
Puttering off like milkweed
In search of more interesting places

Monday, August 17, 2009

Squiggles and wiggles
On the surfaces
Of the tiniest ponds
Turn into the creations
Of the day
As the newly formed dragonflies
Like decimal places on a time sheet
Lift-off in chase
Of the newly formed flies

Monday, August 24, 2009

The nights wrap around the days
Like swaddling cloths
Patterns woven on the fabric
Dance back and forth
Like time sheet entries across the page

Monday, August 31, 2009

Though we were restful
The day moved along
With the impatience of seagulls
That flew just above our heads
And stood right at the edge
Of our blanket
Dashing in on occasion
To try and steal our peanuts
Cutting and chopping
Like scissors through a time sheet

Tuesday, September 8, 2009

Throughout the dental procedure
Mouth agape
Unsatisfied with staring at the dots
On the ceiling panels

Points with no pointillism

I turned my thoughts to teeth
To an old geologist friend
Who used to sift through streambeds for fossils
He had amassed
An amazing collection
Of ancient shark teeth
When he died

Beautiful long petrified things
Curved dark brown and black
With the enamel still intact
And I wanted to ask my dentist
How human teeth would hold up
I wanted to know how well they would fare
In comparison
But I said nothing
As my dentist
Was a distant person
I waited for my receipt
At the receptionist's desk
And folded it when I got it
As it was a large and unruly thing
A full sheet of paper
With almost nothing on it
Like a time sheet
With no entries

Monday, September 14, 2009

Standing in the backyard
On a rainy afternoon
Contemplating overdue home renovations
I sneezed
And sent my temporary crown
Flying into the wet grass

The statistics of finding it
In the three or four foot area
Around where I had been standing
Seemed poor
Like trying to find a misplaced decimal
On a giant time sheet

As the grass was deep
And poorly tended
With small holes
Left by skunks
Digging for grubs

But I persisted on all fours
Until I found it
And then reattached it inside

Looking into the mirror
At the tooth
Without the crown
I was reminded of pictures
Of pre-historic fish teeth
And I laughed to myself
That I was closer to them
Than I realized

Monday, September 21, 2009

And so the summer ended quickly
And decisively
With a crispness in the air
That unmistakably belonged to something else
Already the green leaves
Still on the trees
Were arching and turning
Poised to turn thin
And brittle
The veins fanning out
Raised in relief
As if lines
Delineating indecipherable entries
On an ancient time sheet

Monday, September 28, 2009

Triangles of geese
Fly overhead
On unseen trajectories
Angles both acute
And obtuse
Barking out their goodbyes
Before they've even passed
The moment gone before
The thought has surfaced
Like trying to piece together
Passed days and arrange them
In lines on a time sheet
Both distant and incomprehensible

Monday, October 5, 2009

Drops of rain tap out indiscernible patterns
On yellow leaves pressed to the ground
An inkless typewriter
Hammering out time sheet entries
Unsaved and unrecorded
Submitted to nothing

Monday, October 12, 2009

The light of each day
Shortens
Though the content of what constitutes a day
Does not
Like a time sheet
Folded in half
Then folded over again

Monday, October 19, 2009

At the end of the circus
Hidden technicians
Fire confetti cannons
That fill the stadium
With tiny white rectangles
Of tissue paper

Appearing at first to be suspended

Plain white and thinner
Than a time sheet
They flash like stars
And twist like butterflies
Into the outreached hands
Of everyone

Monday, October 26, 2009

As they danced
In the night of the twenty-first century
There were reminders around them
Of previous times
Artifacts donated by local farmers
Sickles and wooden collars for cattle
Hung from the walls
Along with other remnants
Of processes that had changed
Or ceased all together
As things had progressed

Thin wooden time sheets
The entries on them
Scratched in with an awl
Hung like country signposts
In the corners

Monday, November 2, 2009

Costumed children
With papier-mâché masks
Made of old time sheets
Pressed together with a flour paste
Run up and down
Porch steps
Pausing at the top
With outstretched arms
To receive the joy of the evening

Monday, November 9, 2009

We stood at the entrance to the corn maze
In early November
And listened to the dead stalks
Rattle in the wind
Like distant bird chatter
Eviscerated cobs of corn
Peeked out from yellowed husks
Stray kernels still anchored to the core
Could be seen
Beneath the peeling edges
Like scattered entries
On an abandoned time sheet

Tuesday, December 1, 2009

Old timbers and beams are renewed
For the new office
While cables are drawn
Floors upholstered
And walls rise
To meet gleaming granite counters
Made from the compression
And hardening
Of layers of time sheets
Fossilized by the ages

Monday, December 7, 2009

Water flows past the sluices
Beneath the building
To unknown destinations
While ducks and geese
Idly turn and dive

A layer of ice
Thinner than a time sheet
Begins to form
At the pond's center

Tuesday, December 15, 2009

Though the paper is thicker than traditional
A discarded time sheet
That has fulfilled its duty
As a historical record
May be put to use again
In concealing smaller presents
And can bring satisfaction
To those who revel in detail

As there are those who appreciate
Crisply folded edges
That stay in place
And an opacity
And resistance to tearing
Second to none

Monday, December 21, 2009

I was surprised
As the snowblower
Pulled itself along the driveway
For the first major storm
By how dry and intact
The fall leaves were
Underneath the snow

Crisp and brittle notations
As to what the weather had been
Nature's own discarded time sheet

Monday, December 28, 2009

I am often surprised
By the stoutness of gift bags
Their glossy paper
Seems to hide materials of a more serious construction
Perhaps it is that
They are inevitably garnished
With the lightest of materials
Crumpled time sheets and tissue papers
Rakishly sticking out
Of the top
Like a paper explosion
Caught as it unfolds

Tuesday, January 5, 2010

Miraculously quickly
The single digits of the century
Had disappeared
And it was suddenly twenty-ten
A time that even in name
Was irrefutably modern
A time in which it was hard to imagine
That such a thing
As simple and as plain
As a paper time sheet
Could ever have been

Monday, January 11, 2010

The boxes and envelopes
And tiny strips of paper
Stick together in clumps
The blue bins themselves
Glued together

As though a massive papier-mâché snow cone
With a base of discarded time sheets
Molded into awkward shapes
Waiting for the sun to somehow recycle everything

Tuesday, January 19, 2010

By evening
The paw prints left in the driveway
From a neighborhood cat
Had become more of a fossilized record
In the ice
Firm enough
So as to have false airs of permanence
As though an inked stamp
On a time sheet
Detailing past arrivals and departures

Monday, January 25, 2010

The rain came down
Not in sheets
But in reams
Cutting and pitting
The snow
Beneath it
Etching out
A brief historical record
Marking the time
In the thinning ice
Like a mechanical punch
On a time sheet

Monday, February 1, 2010

There are gray days
Or perhaps series of gray days
Long enough
That it almost seems supernatural
When the sun is suddenly seen
Unexpected in the afternoon
High and bright and full
Completely unobstructed
Towering over and through
The buildings below

So surprising and strong in its manner
That an unfinished room
Not yet fitted with blinds
Set with little more than a desk
And a pile of time sheets

Even the unfinished room
Seems surprised

Monday, February 8, 2010

There is something primal in ticker tape celebrations
A temporary release of all anxiety
A seemingly simple snowstorm
Of shredded paper
That falls slowly
As though to preserve some essence
Of the very records and time sheets
That were not preserved
But rather
Turned loose from great heights
To find their way in a new form

Stephen R Wagner

Monday, February 15, 2010

It is often the case
That one thing is muddled as another
A note on a time sheet
Perhaps
Indicating that the time
Should have in fact
Been billed to something else

Or a holiday
Celebrating all the presidents
That is really more a celebration
Of the original president
Choosing not
To be a king

Monday, February 22, 2010

Spring presses up
Through the edges and ends of winter
Like a seed that has begun to germinate
Beneath discarded time sheets
Left dirty and weather-worn on the ground

Monday, March 1, 2010

As I sat in bed trying to coax
My little girl to sleep during a rainstorm
I listened to the wind and reflected on the fact
That it did not howl
But rather sounded like a jet
Passing constantly overhead
And it made me think
Directly of time sheets now
How far removed from a sheet they actually are
At their essence
A series of 1s and 0s
Decipherable only to the machines

Tuesday, March 9, 2010

It is amazing how quickly
Objects bend and blend back into nature
The eighty-feet of fallen fence in the backyard
At first highly noticeable and out of place
Quickly camouflages itself to the eye
Resting comfortably
Amid the yellow patches of lawn
That have not yet caught up with spring

The planks soften daily
Giving way to the ground beneath them
A mulchy time sheet for the ants
And other creatures

Tuesday, March 16, 2010

Trying to wait out the storm
That seemed to last days longer than it should
It was impossible not to incessantly check
The ceilings and floors
Staring at nothing
Looking for gradual darkening spots to appear

Like processing a blank time sheet with a lemon
Looking for swirls of invisible ink
To come into view

Monday, March 22, 2010

Pulling the trash out to the curb
In the gloomy early morning light
Waiting for the rain to start
I heard the geese call as they passed over me
And had to catch myself
As it took a minute
To realize that the birds were not disappearing
But rather returning
For a moment the information would not register
It was like trying to change an entry
On a time sheet already submitted
To retrieve a letter already sent

Monday, March 29, 2010

Working to separate a single coffee filter
From the stack in an early morning fight
I was struck by the similarity
Of coffee filters and time sheets
Incredibly thin slips of paper
That somehow work to filter the original
Inedible contents
Ground coffee dust
And the days blurring into nights
Into something palatable and quickly understood
Liquid vitality and a map of the essence of time

Monday, April 5, 2010

When I got home from work on Friday night
My daughter was crying, nearly inconsolable
She had picked on a whim a tiny crocus
That had popped up in the center of the yard
And she had quickly wanted to put it back
My wife had tried to explain that they could not
That it could not
And unfortunately, perhaps, she had understood
And was crying
Saying that she wanted it to start over again
What could we do?
I eventually brought her back
To the patch of wild crocuses
And we gently returned our charge
Which was nothing more now than a stem
Barely thicker than a hair
With a few purple petals above it
We placed it back among the others
And I propped it up slightly
With some leaves that had fallen nearby
As I had realized that I could not
Or perhaps I would not force her to see yet
What was irreversible
We chose that day not to stare at the picked state
Of the flower
The unalterable aspect
Of the submitted time sheet
Available for editing or adjustment no more
We chose instead to trust in the unusual
Implausible possibility of things

Monday, April 12, 2010

Of course, there is always more to the story

Behind the scenes details
As when an engineer can't submit their time sheet
Because they are eagerly awaiting
The birth of a new project

Or significant preceding details
As it turns out that my wife
Had extensively warned our daughter
That to pick a flower
Would set in motion a one-way set of events

But she had not been able to resist

Monday, May 3, 2010

There is a depression in my front yard
That I can't seem to keep filled
I've tried leaves and grass seeds
Even full sheets of sod
But nothing seems to take
It is almost as if I'm working
In a web browser
On a form or a time sheet
And I keep navigating away
Before I can save my changes

Monday, May 10, 2010

In an effort to take advantage of the yard
We built raised garden beds
And populated them with seedlings
Lined up in rows like one's and two's
Across a time sheet
Tiny entries on a broad canvas

Standing there
Staring down at them
It was hard to fathom
How much they would soon grow

Monday, May 17, 2010

With a flurry of modernization
We've moved to automate the yard
Embedding soaker hoses on timers
In the strawberry patch
Along the driveway
And in the raised beds out back
Tying our tiny plots of seedlings and loose dirt
Into the sprawling water grid
As though we were synching the data
On our electronic time sheets
Through the cloud
To the servers that lay beyond

Monday, May 25, 2010

It is during the process of training new engineers
In the time keeping system
When I warn them
Of the dangers of falling behind
How difficult it can be
To try and recreate more than just a few days
On paper
That I sometimes think of my oldest daughter
And how I'll often chat to her
About something funny
Or irreverent
That happened the day before
Only to discover that, at three
She often has no recollection
Of the idle things mentioned
And I am forced to realize
That much of these first few years
That we have spent together
Will be entirely forgotten
It will be pieced together only
Through the scattershot photos and home films
That have been taken randomly
And strung together over the years
Along with the few and specific anecdotes
Of the most irreverent moments
That we choose to keep
By telling and retelling them
To keep them present
It is through this and these
That we will piece together our time sheets
The best we can

Tuesday, June 1, 2010

The 'Mammoth Russian' sunflowers
That we planted from seed
From nothing almost
Quickly rose from their raised beds
Though it must have taken them
The requisite seven-to-ten days
To germinate

It seemed that it couldn't really have been
More than two or three

Now they are well on their way
To half-a-foot
And are budgeted to rise to twelve
But it is hard to envision this
As we still tower over them

They sway in their early stages
Like single entries
On an earthen time sheet

Monday, June 7, 2010

As workloads surge
Like flashfloods in a culvert
So too the time sheets swell
From severe storms

Tuesday, June 15, 2010

It is fun sometimes
For me to see the analogies and equivalences
Between the time keeping process
And the real life lived

In order to ferry the girls across town
On bicycles
Under grayish skies
That may turn either way
We must first fasten down child seats
To the frames
And hitch a trailer
That runs behind
To accommodate
Any possible combination
Of children and groceries

The booking of the project
As it were
Before we may enter the data
On our time sheets

Monday, June 28, 2010

I don't visit the seedlings
As often as I should

But when I do I have to smile
As they waver back and forth
With the undulations of the air

Like guests at a party
Rocking back and forth on their heels
Crowded in for conversation
Clustered like numbers
Cascading
Across a time sheet

Tuesday, July 6, 2010

We had giant shrimp for dinner
That still had their small
Walking and swimming legs attached
And it made me realize
That I had forgotten
The existence of such things
The legs gone from the shrimp
Just as the hands of the workers
Have shrunken from view
Having stared so long
Across long flat planes of numbers
Running over time sheets

Monday, July 12, 2010

At the beginning of the summer
When we'd let the grass grow
Half as high as the children
And then had to catch up with the mowing
I'd noticed hoards of tiny white insects
Surging away as I passed
Like spray from the surf
Or tiny white sparks
That emanated from the machine itself
I had assumed them to be tiny gnats
Or midges
Or some other nuisance creature
But when my oldest daughter came into the yard
To check on things as I was finishing up
We decided to stop and crouch down in the grass
To look more closely
And we discovered that the tiny creatures
Were in fact miniature grasshoppers
Fully formed but incredibly small
Jumping away from us
Visible in the air for only a second
Arching away like decimal places
Jumping off a time sheet
Into oblivion

Monday, July 19, 2010

Standing back in the library area
Of the office
Looking out to the pond
The individual window panes
Divide the scene outside into segments

Like cells on a time sheet
The geese standing on a separate plane
From the lily pads

Tuesday, July 27, 2010

The minutes of the day
Ripple across the surface
Of our time sheet
Shining as they shift
Disappearing like water
Under the prow of the boat

Tuesday, August 2, 2010

When the baby had trouble
Getting settled on the pontoon boat
I brought her to the prow of the boat
And held her in the crook of my arm

Swaddled in her life vest
She looked out to the water over the rail
And grew restful
As we watched the boats passing around us
And the trees along the shore

And I thought of how her mind
Was transforming all of the sights and sounds
Into the human equivalent of ones and zeroes
The binary of the mind
The coding behind the time sheet
The notes and job information
Turned into simple raw numbers
The root level of the language of the machines

Tuesday, August 9, 2010

It is fascinating to see
How the fruit flies once established
Seem to spring from almost nothing

A simple flourish of an arm
Above a pile of time sheets
Causes three or four to take to the air
Lurching upwards and away
On wobbly trajectories

As though the numbers on the sheets themselves
Had woken from an ancient slumber
To drone off across the office
Following some timeless instinctual signal

Monday, August 23, 2010

When the grill had come to temperature
I turned and saw the heat waves
Rippling over a plastic deck table
A few feet away
Constant motion from left to right

As though the heat were moving
Horizontally instead of rising
Like a shallow stream passing over
The river bed just beneath it

Like a breath across a time sheet
Blowing away tiny traces of eraser
Almost too small to be seen

Monday, August 30, 2010

As hurricanes form along the coasts
Riptides pull at the beaches
Sharpening the angles of the dunes
The image of the time sheet itself
Wavers on the screen
Due to problems
Down along the lines

Monday, September 13, 2010

I had thought prior to the trip
That seeing the whales
Breach the surface of the water
Would provide a good metaphor for numbers
Emerging on the surface of a time sheet

But I was the first one to throw up
Over the railing
As we raced to find the whales at 25 knots
In four-foot swells
Our one-year-old
Was in the process of throwing up
On the shirt of a family friend
When I returned from the deck
So I took our three-year-old in my arms
To comfort her amid the confusion
Whereupon she threw up voluminously
Over the two of us
And then fell into a furtive sleep on my lap
As our clothes dried and hardened
My wife held out the longest
But finally succumbed across the aisle
While I took turns sharing the bucket
In front of our bench with the younger girls

At some point I heard on the intercom
We had reached the whales
I briefly saw a black fin
Through the dirty acrylic window
But was unable to turn beyond that
As our pod clutched the tables
With eyes closed to make it through
Blank time sheets on a dark screen

Monday, September 20, 2010

The final weekend of the season
Steeped in languishing sun
A chance for the lawn chairs and umbrellas
To be put away
Exposed window sills painted
The inflatable pool drained and folded
A project complete
Time sheets submitted invoiced and paid in full
Poised for a status change from active to inactive

Monday, September 27, 2010

I was lying in the yard
Waiting for my youngest daughter
To retrieve a ball
That had rolled beyond reach
When I looked to the weeds around me
And noticed the characteristics
Of a stalk of crabgrass
How it was almost a militarized version
Of a regular blade of grass
Thicker and taller
Joined with encased glossy blades
Spreading out rakishly from a central base
And I was contemplating tearing it out
At the roots
When I noticed it had tiny purple flowers
At the top
Arched and fuzzy not even so large as a single eyelash
And it was like finding something
That shouldn't exist
Something terribly incongruous
Like magnifying the numeric data
In the cells of a time sheet
Only to find tiny creatures
Toiling on the edges of the pixels
Busily engaged in anything
But the keeping of time

Monday, October 4, 2010

Although it is likely that the days
Have dimmed gradually and consistently
Losing light incrementally
It does not feel so

Rather it is as though the brightness
And contrast of the monitor
And the day
Had suddenly been reduced
To almost nothing
Making the time sheet on the screen
Nearly indiscernible

Monday, October 11, 2010

Having begun to wander from the camp
Down a path in the dark
I looked up to the night and saw
That the mid sections of the trees above me
Were illuminated by a white light
Cast from a lantern back at the site

Small ovular deciduous leaves
Like flattened pears that had not yet fallen
Caught the light twenty feet above me
And glowed ghostly white
Against the black backdrop of the upper canopy

Like small warped zeroes
Electric white
Suspended
In the heart of a pure black time sheet

Monday, October 18, 2010

It is only now at the height of fall
That I am able to fully appreciate the season

Though the light of early mornings
And late afternoons
Has been taken from us
We are compensated
With bursts of windy light
At the heart of days

A briskness that passes over the time sheets
Making the numerals stand out in relief

Monday, October 25, 2010

The only things that emerge from the rain
And the traffic of the early morning commute
Are the trees that have lost all green
Turned instead
To raucous oranges reds and yellows
That seem to be lighted from within

As though a switch had been thrown
To allow the power through

Sudden and arresting
Like a change of font on the time sheets
Switching from black to gold

Monday, November 1, 2010

Picking up around the house before guests arrived
I was struck by the remarkable locations
Of all the toys and household things
Items left at all levels of reaching
Balls, puzzle pieces, remotes
Dropped pieces of food
Over, under
And on top of everything
As though a great tide had risen
And then receded
Leaving things strewn about
As if the numbers on the bottom of a time sheet
Had been knocked loose by a great wave
And swept to the top
Numbers left on their sides and upside down
Amid the seaweed of scrambled line borders

Monday, November 8, 2010

When the time change finally comes
Its effects are infinitely larger than expected
It would not seem likely that a single hour
Could make the sky so dark
Or the day so long
And yet it does

As though a hundred line items
Had been added to the time sheet
Pushing the end down off the screen
Beyond view
Unscrollable

Monday, November 15, 2010

Though it has yet to snow this season
There was a sense of it
In the air over the weekend
And so I began to clear the driveway
Of leaves and debris
Old boards and dirt
Moving the barrels to the edge of the yard
To make room for the snow
Clearing all of the lines and numbers
Off of the time sheet itself
Leaving only the white

Monday, November 22, 2010

This fall I surprised the uncut grass
And fallen leaves
By not allowing them to become encased
In the season's first snow

But rather I mowed everything
To tiny pieces
In the mid-November air

Cutting all of the old, overgrown projects
And line entries
Off of the sprawling time sheet
Leaving only the core group
Of new live-growth hours beneath

Monday, November 29, 2010

It is still clearly fall
But the water bottle on the rabbits' hutch
Is beginning to freeze up most nights

And the frost on the car's windshield
Is taking longer and longer
To melt in the morning

It will soon be time to bring everything in
And batten down the hatches
To add a layer of glass over the time sheets
To seal off and insulate
The numbers growing within

Monday, December 6, 2010

I do not fully understand the geese and ducks
They had left the pond out back
Behind the mill
During the summer
Which seemed reasonable enough
But they've returned recently
Although the weather's worsened

It seems strange
As though an incorrect selection
Has been made on a time sheet

Having chosen personal/sick time
Perhaps
Instead of vacation
Cold climate over warm
And then not realizing
Or acknowledging the error

Monday, December 13, 2010

Sometimes it seems that
It is only through the occurrence
Of small damages that events are traceable

The scratch on the wooden floor
From the Christmas tree stand
The worn veneer on the dinner chair
Where the booster seat
Had been strapped for years

A vacation note tied to billable work
On a time sheet
By mistake

Monday, December 20, 2010

Although the first snow of the season
May arrive in the form
Of a calm and gentle dusting
It does not matter
People will drive in the first storm
Like rabid animals
That have been locked inside cars

Oblivious into oblivion
As if the monitors displaying their time sheets
Had descended into a frenzied strobe
Throwing the viewers into shocks and fits

Monday, January 3, 2011

It seems amazing on some level
That we've reached the year twenty-eleven
As it still sounds far off and unattainable

It is luck perhaps
That the machines themselves
Keep such good time
As the software advances the current time sheet
To the next week and the next year
Regardless of where the user stands

Monday, January 10, 2011

The buildings
On a PowerPoint slide
Of the city
Rise in an aerial view
Like red gray and brown iron shavings
That have been drawn upwards
Magnetically charged
Against the black backdrop
Of the water around them
Coaxed towards the sky
As though the numbers on a time sheet
Had been commanded to stand up
And did

Wednesday, January 19, 2011

Looking out the office windows
To the pond below
Before the snowfall had turned to rain
I was surprised to see
How large the snowflakes could be
I had forgotten the range of snow
And the possible contrast

Like seeing a twelve hour day
On a time sheet
That normally holds eights

Monday, January 24, 2011

On the one hand perhaps
It's simply been a little snowier
And colder than usual
But on the other
At some deeper level
It feels like we might be getting a glimpse
Of a fundamental shift
In the nature and severity of weather itself

As though watching the characters and numerals
On the time sheets before us
Briefly change to some entirely other
Unintelligible script and then return
Pulsing in and out of coherence

Monday, January 31, 2011

The front porch has disappeared into the snow
While slush piles press against the house
And ice dams force water under the shingles
Like bamboo under a fingernail
The yard has been consumed by whitespace
As though a single-sided time sheet
Flipped over to reveal the blank underneath

Monday, February 7, 2011

Adding insulation to the old rock wool
Between the joists in the attic
Some fiberglass fibers got past my gloves
And worked their way into my fingers
Causing me to reflect
On how well they were named
As they felt exactly like little fibers of glass

As aptly named as the time sheet
A flat singular plane
Attempting to simulate the passage of time
With nothing more
Than descriptive characters and numerals

Monday, February 14, 2011

As intractable and permanent
As winter seemed a few days before
With a brief pause in snowfall
And a mild rise in temperature
It again seems surmountable

It is no longer entirely inconceivable
That we will be leveling the dirt
And inflating the kiddie pools
Five months from now

A season shift with the possibility
Of different projects and entries
On the time sheets to come

Monday, February 21, 2011

As I went down
To return some tools
To the basement
My daughter called to me through the cat door
Within the larger door
At the top of the stairs

She said
"It's not going to last forever, you know."
I turned to see her small face
Pressed against the cat door
And asked, "What's not going to last forever?"
"The World," she said

I couldn't help but laughing
"Perhaps"
I thought
But for now at least
There are time sheets to be entered
And entries to be submitted
So it goes

Monday, March 7, 2011

On the eve of an extended stay-cation
Having been sick all week
It was unclear
How I would muster the energy required
For the major renovations
Due to start next day

In the end
I made the beds and began to tidy
Picking up scattered items
Throughout the house

When I paused and took stock of things
I realized that I was sick
But that I was ready

It turns out
That when you turn the stereo to twenty-five
You can feel it in the very timbers of the house
The time sheet entries become simple
Work work work work

Monday, March 14, 2011

With the sprawling chain
Of natural and unnatural disasters
Writhing across the ocean
I crouched in my basement
Wearing goggles, gloves and a respirator
And labored to apply heavy oil-based stains evenly
I was surprised
To hear a single goose heading north
Call out from far above the bulkhead doors
Spring it seems would come regardless

Monday, March 21, 2011

Visiting my father's house with my girls
I was surprised to find that he had captured
A squirrel
Which he needed us to release
Unsure where to go
We brought the squirrel home
To our own house and released it in the backyard
It disappeared across the yard
A gray blur into the trees
I quietly wondered if this squirrel
Having broken into my father's house
Had become militarized and would be more likely
To break into my own
A strange gray entry on an odd time sheet

Monday, March 28, 2011

We keep an old shelter-rabbit
In the basement during the winter
Tonight perhaps we will bring him above ground
For the season
To the larger hutch in the yard
With the fenced-in-run

We've placed a plank that leads from the hutch
To the ground
But the rabbit is too timid or old to use it
We must remember to lower him to the yard
And return him at night
A daily task
The filling out of his time sheet
With notations that spring has truly begun

Monday, April 4, 2011

Merging onto the highway in the morning
During the final snowstorm of the year
I encountered a convoy of enormous trucks
Fitted with giant plows
Like baleen

Blue electric whales
Moving slowly in staggered formation
Along the lanes
Like dinosaurs forced into migration
Creatures at the end of the film
Returning to Monster Island
All time entered
All submissions complete

Monday, April 11, 2011

We hauled eight, 30-gallon bags of leaves
To the town compost site
And the joke
Was that the yard didn't look any better
But we'd broken ground
Sprinkled milkweed seeds
And buried an echinacea taproot
To summon the butterflies
As though submitting a proposal to nature
Bidding on a prospective job
In the fall perhaps we will mark our time sheets
With the births and launchings of monarchs

Monday, April 18, 2011

The bottom of the fire pit
Rusted away during the winter
From the moisture held by last year's coals
But it's sound enough to still contain fires
Allowing us to burn the old fence pieces
We couldn't sneak into the trash
Clearing the yard of old projects
Old time entries
On old time sheets
From the past

Monday, April 25, 2011

As a last minute detail
Before the children came downstairs
I dipped a stuffed animal's paw
Into foot deodorizing powder
And made tracks leading up to the loot

Tangible evidence
A mark on our time sheet
Indicating the passage of mythical creatures

Monday, May 2, 2011

It turns out that there is a place in Newburyport
That inspects motorcycles until 3 p.m. on Saturdays
I made it and finalized the paperwork
Of legitimizing the tiniest motorcycle
Or perhaps the largest moped
I had ever ridden

While I waited in the shop for the inspection
I asked if they worked on small bikes like these
And the owner said, "It depends."
And dragged out the words in a funny way

I knew in a second
That he had nothing but contempt for the bike

But he did not know the joys
Of the discontinued
Company extinct
2010 Fly Scout 110cc motorcycle
Produced by the fine folks
At the Yinxiang Motorcycle Group
In mainland China

He did not know
That an awesome time sheet adventure
Of incalculable proportions had just begun

He was a silly man

Monday, May 9, 2011

What is miraculous
Is that our elderly shelter-rabbit
Who had a miserable personality
When we first got him a few years ago
Has changed

Due in large part
To my youngest daughter
Who feeds him
Prodigiously
And sits with him
In his pen

Many mornings
When she wakes up
She points to the window
And says emphatically, "bunny, bunny, bunny,"
Until we take her out

The bunny has responded
He runs to her and sits patiently
While she works at petting him

It has been tremendous to witness

A massive restructuring
Of intransigent locked-down time sheet entries
Moved and transformed
At a higher administrative level

Monday, May 16, 2011

Halfway through the process
Of making a periscope
For the fort
I am reminded
Of all the complexities

All of the trial
And error
Of renovating
From scratch

A process in which
Success seems implausible
At best
For a tremendously
Long period of time
Until suddenly it's imminent

And I know
Even though I don't know it yet
That we'll soon be able to peer
From the first floor
To the second
To scan the yard for both
Friend and foe
From one time sheet
To the next

Monday, May 23, 2011

The rain is interminable
Magical in its effect
To make difficult things
More difficult

Gloomy
Time sheet entries
Gloomier

Tuesday, May 31, 2011

Halfway through filling
Last year's sixty dollar pool
A leak was detected
That jeopardized the integrity
Of the entire project

Without delay
I retrieved my tube
Of Mr. Sticky's Underwater Aquarium Glue
And for this
For being prepared
For the possibility
Of a system failure
Having purchased the glue
Years before
And never used it
Knowing only that it could come in handy
At some future unknown point in time

I am indebted to my father
From whom I have learned
To collect and gather
Useful things
The ultimate
Time-keeping administrator
Available to charge time
To any and all projects
Across all time sheets
Though few projects
May ever be charged against
The capacity
Is there

Wednesday, June 8, 2011

With the good weather
Having finally firmly arrived
Somehow it is suddenly
June
And the year
Is half over

The days clatter along
Like freight cars
Coupled together
Doors open
With time sheets
Loose
On the floors of the cars

Monday, June 13, 2011

We ended up going out to eat
At a restaurant on the beach
And couldn't resist
Going down
To the sand

It was rainy and gray
And the girls got water
In their boots
But the ocean was still magnificent
Immune to the trivialities
And fluctuations
Of time sheets

Monday, June 20, 2011

Box turtles
From the ravine behind our house
Laid their eggs in the front lawn
A few weeks ago
And most of the eggs
Were dug up and eaten
But I believe
That a few survived
And that a few of those
Will hatch
And go about their business
Governed by
Tiny time sheets
With all entries
Focused on survival

Monday, June 27, 2011

Standing by the sink
On Sunday evening
Cutting up the plastic rings
From a six-pack

It occurred to me
How strange it was
That the rings
Often end up
In the ocean

All the countless small pieces
Bobbing
Like individual time sheet entries
Adrift on
The Great Pacific Trash Vortex

Tuesday, July 5, 2011

Avoiding the crowds
And the parking concerns
Of the main field
From which the Independence fireworks
Were launched
We watched instead
Further away
On a hill
From the parking lot
Behind the modest
British Colonial Apartments
Sitting on bundled piles
Of construction materials
The irony
Seemed to be lost
On the crowd
Who were rightly
More concerned
With the modification
Of the week's time sheet
A Monday more filled
With lawn chairs and glow sticks
Than anything else

Monday, July 11, 2011

And somehow
We've reached
The heart of summer
Water-balloon fights
Finally present themselves
As good ideas
Sprinklers become
More entertaining
And unbillable hours
Of lounging by the pool
Bookend busier time sheet entries

Monday, July 18, 2011

Driving to work
On my bike
Down the small back roads
That run along the river
I came across
Two small flocks of wild turkeys
That milled about in the road
Before disappearing
Into the underbrush
It was remarkable
How enjoyable it was
To catch a glimpse
Of wild things that live along the cusp
Of the forest
A fantastical border
Seen from the edge
Of my time sheet

Monday, July 25, 2011

Molly our older cat
Disappeared on Monday
And it was clear to me as the days passed
That she'd been eaten
By creatures in the ravine

She had always been
Slightly off

Rescued as a kitten
From a house of ninety-nine cats
She was one of the few with both eyes

It took us years to become brave enough
To let her out
But when we did she flourished
Until she disappeared

And it was with great surprise
That we found her
Sunday evening
Alive and well
In our own house
Let in by a neighbor
Shortly before we returned
From a weekend away
Proof that no matter
As to any and all
Projections that are made
The actual events
On the time sheets before us
May simply not be known
Ahead of their occurrence

Monday, August 1, 2011

Just beyond the bridge where most people
Pull their canoes out of the river
A police officer kept watch
All day Sunday
"It's been a good day so far,"
He told our group
No one had been arrested
Yet

By the giant dumpster
Filled with torn floats and rafts
A man worked ceaselessly
To process the endless stream of bottles and cans
Being brought up from the boats

Industrial sized transparent bags
Filled with empties
Bags taller than I
And wider than the stretch of my arms
Formed a wall around him
Hiding him from view
Obscuring the activities
Of a weekend
Time sheet

Friday, August 5, 2011 (For Monday)

Tonight
I send you a reminder
Before the event has even
Occurred
As I will be off the coast tomorrow
Navigating the craggy rocks
That line the tide pools
At the edge of the ocean
Hunting for creatures
Alongside my own
Creatures

I will not be thinking
About your
Time sheets

Monday, August 15, 2011

There is always
A brief moment of panic
When your two-year-old
Starts vomiting grapes
Along the rocks
On an island
That boldly states
The impossibility of medical attention
But even this
May be assuaged
By the healing power
Of a good nap
Along with the careful
Administration of whoopie pies
Prescribed with gelatos
Cold beers
And hot seafood
Taken along the water's edge

Monday, August 22, 2011

While we will never know
The true causal nature of any chain of events
It is fun to conjecture
As to the curvature of the path

The other morning
Our two cats fought wildly on the stairs
As though electrified
So I let the older one out
And left the house myself a few minutes later
To find the cat walking around our car
With a dead blue jay
Hanging from its mouth

I gently shook the cat's back
And the bird fell from her mouth
Righted itself in the air and flew strongly off
Without ever brushing
The ground below
While it had been dangling
Just short of lifeless
The moment before

A time sheet changed
In an instant

Tuesday, September 6, 2011

At the height
Of the afternoon heat
My four-year-old
Dug out a fancy dress
And some fancy shoes

And we both put on
Wide-brimmed hats

And wandered around the neighborhood
Plucking tiny weedy-flowers
From the sidewalk

Studying things
Through an oversized orange
Magnifying glass
We remarked to each other
What good use of our time sheets
We were making

Monday, September 12, 2011

Though they sit dormant and idle
Forgotten most of the year
It is now as the summer wanes
That we light the torches
Bolted to the back deck
To push back the night

Ten torches bolted to the banisters
Evenly spaced around the perimeter
Press back the darkness
And lift the cold

The deck rails turn to feudal ramparts
As the torches reach out
With foot high flames
Of burning oil
Hearkening back
To more ancient times
Simpler time sheets
The transitioning of the seasons

Things that are not seen
But felt

Monday, September 19, 2011

Having paddled down
The placid Connecticut River
All morning
We clambered out of our boats
At the predetermined end of our trip
And scrambled up the banks
Up twenty feet or so
To a grass plateau
Where we ate
A welcome hot meal

The mud at the edge of the plateau
Was wet and deeply cracked
As the river had been raging
At that height just a few weeks prior

A visual testament
To the variant events
That mark the passage of time
Swinging wildly from one time sheet
To the next

Stephen R Wagner

Monday, September 26, 2011

We welcomed in the fall
By cleaning the moss and mildew
Off of the side of the house

I'd been meaning to test a theory
Over the last five or six years
As to whether the mildew
Would come off with some soapy water
And a gentle scrubbing with a moist time sheet
And it turns out it does
Amazing

Monday, October 3, 2011

Most weekday mornings
Around six-thirty
As I perform my morning chores
My littlest one
Cecelia
Works her way
Down the stairs
In her pajamas
To check on me
And after we've settled
The matter of getting some juice
We head into the sunroom
To feed the fish
And as she lifts the superworm she's selected
From the container
It inevitably curls around her finger
And she calls out, "It tickle me!"
Before she drops it into the tank

After some additional pellets
To round out the nutrition
We're done feeding the fish
And I lower her to the ground

One tiny thing
Completed
One tiny task
On one tiny time sheet
Done

Tuesday, October 11, 2011

I initially caught the flying squirrel
In our bedroom
Guided by the cats around 5 a.m.

I placed it in an animal carrier
And brought it down to our mudroom
To be addressed
When we got up for the day
But of course
By then the flying squirrel
Had chewed through the carrier and was loose

So I put the heavy-duty dish washing gloves
Back on
And brought one of the cats
Into the mudroom to help rout it out
While my wife and children
Watched through the closed glass door

It was when the squirrel
Jumped onto my face
That my wife started laughing

After several more minutes
Of struggling and biting
The squirrel was eventually recaptured
And relocated in the repaired carrier
To the woods far away

A strange and unpredictable time sheet
Punctuated with the wildness
That only small woodland creatures
May bring

Monday, October 17, 2011

On a didactic hayride
At a local farm
We learned that coyotes
Walk patiently
Behind the combines
As they harvest the crops

Catching the small creatures
That emerge
To flee from the machines

Filling out their time sheets
Lazily in the sun

Monday, October 24, 2011

I took the girls to the beach
While the sun was still out
And we poked around in the sand
Until we found a buoy
That had washed up on the jetty rocks

We all got excited

The lobster trap was long gone
But the buoy still had a long wet rope attached
So I dragged the rope
Back and forth
Along the sharp edge of a rock
Like an escapee cutting his bonds
Until the rope broke
And we clambered up the beach
With our prize

And my oldest daughter who is four
Kept saying
"I can't believe we found a real buoy."
"I'm so happy."
"I'm just so happy."

And she wanted to show
Everyone we met and tell them
How we had cut the rope
But I was a little concerned
That people might see it
Out of context
It was a day well spent
Time sheets filled
With thoroughly rounded entries

Monday, October 31, 2011

When I was growing up
The internet had yet to be deployed
And our first computer had cartridges
That needed to be jammed
Into the back of the keyboard
Everything was entirely text based

And now my two-year-old is shouting
From the bottom of the stairs
"I want to play 'puter games, Daddy!"
And she spends more time
On the iPod than I do

Hers will be a virtual time sheet
Unrecognizable to me

Monday, November 7, 2011

I was standing with my four-year-old
At the dining room table
Between activities
Wiping something or other
Off of the tabletop

When she said to me
In a very clear and explanatory tone
"If it couldn't, it wouldn't."

I questioned her
As to whether
She was referring
To something that preceded
Her statement

But it stood alone
Tied to nothing

How true, I thought
"If it could not, then how would it?"

It was going to be a very complex
And interesting
Time sheet

Monday, November 14, 2011

We returned to the beach
And found an entire lobster pot
Buried
With only the lid visible
Uncovered by scavengers with metal detectors
We dug in and around the lobster pot
For some time
It appeared to be new
With the parts intact
And after some digging
We reached the top of the bait bag

And I started to wonder
If we would make a macabre find
Of mummified lobsters
But the pot was firmly buried
And it was too much for our little group
As we were not equipped with shovels

So we gave up but went instead
To have an impromptu lobster lunch
On a deck
Suspended just above the ocean
The wine and the water
Sparkling in splashes of late fall sun

The working portion of the day's time sheet
Done

Monday, November 21, 2011

We made a leaf pile
Taller than the children
And it drew them in
Like metal filings
To a super-magnet

Countless leaves
Churning
One over the next
Lost pieces
Of a deciduous time sheet

Monday, November 28, 2011

At the aquarium
Through triple-paned glass
We watched a scuba diver
Quietly scrub the back
Of an old sea turtle
While hundreds of fish
Swirled around and around
Above them

A time sheet entry
Twenty-three feet
Below the sea

Monday, December 5, 2011

I stood at the edge of the carpeted enclosure
Where the older girls were dancing
In celebration of their princess party
I was holding my two-year-old and I asked her
If I should put her down so she could join them

But she looked at me and said
"There's a lot of kids in there."
So we held back a little longer
Watching them dance
Running and squiggling
Across their time sheets

Monday, December 12, 2011

With the water bottle
Starting to freeze
More regularly
We finally moved the rabbit
From his outdoor hutch
To the basement hutch
A true sign
Of the change of seasons
Outdoor time sheets
Suspended until further notice

Monday, December 19, 2011

One of the cats passed me
Late at night
In the hallway
On its way
Somewhere

And I suddenly realized
How cleverly
Cats
Had positioned themselves
To people

Domesticated
Just enough
To be allowed to roam free
Anywhere
To return to shelter
At will

No time sheets
None
At all

Tuesday, December 27, 2011

Of all the presents
It was the stickers
That got my attention
Sprawling art sets
That boasted total piece counts
In the thousands
1300 stickers in one set alone
Approximately 1800 in another

Tiny highly adhesive stickers
Concentrated on rolls
That the children unfurled
And deployed everywhere

Working in frantic over-time
On their time sheets
Spreading out across the room
Rapidly placing one sticker
On top of another higgledy-piggledy
As though there were little time

Tuesday, January 3, 2012

Impossibly another year has gone by
Everything faster
Not just the experiences
But the very modes of communication
The exchanges
And still the winter has yet to set in
Biding its time sheets
Until we've forgotten what very cold is

Monday, January 9, 2012

The children are obsessed
With pieces of ice
That have formed in the backyard
Small blocks
That have taken the shapes
Of the various containers
Lying around

Small toys and leaves
Stick out rakishly

The children check them
Compulsively
Like doctors on their rounds
Filling out their time sheets
With the details
Of their patients' progress

Monday, January 16, 2012

I brought my girls
To visit their grandfather's house
Late on a Saturday afternoon
So they could see
The clutter
And the teetering piles

After a reluctant tour
The girls wanted to show my father
Pictures they had drawn

But there was nowhere
In the sprawling three-story house
That four people could sit down together

So the girls sat on my lap
In a tattered chair
And my father stood nearby
While they went over the drawings
And the stories behind them

While all around us
Things loomed

The equivalent of a billion
Empty time sheets
Bundled together

Nothing
Being carefully preserved
For the benefit
Of no one

Monday, January 23, 2012

Both girls came alive
Linguistically
Between the ages of two and three
And this is where
Cecelia is now
The other day
In the dim morning light
I was preparing things in the kitchen
When she called to me
From the top of the stairs
So I brought her down and returned to my chores
With her nestled on my arm
When she turned my face to hers
With both hands
Leaned in close
And said
"You want to shee something cray-shee?"
I nodded
And she directed me
Into the living room
Where we saw
The cat
Eating my cereal

Something crazy indeed
A time sheet
Crammed full
Of observations

Monday, January 30, 2012

The water
Sitting in the pots
In the backyard
Can't decide
If it's fluid or solid
As it transforms back
Again and again
Confused by the abnormal weather
A winter time sheet
Filled with corrections
Scribbled over
With notes

Monday, February 6, 2012

As we were leaving the supermarket
My oldest daughter called up
To the inflatable display by the door
"Good luck, baseball-player man."

We watched some of the game that night
And she was obsessed with the score
When we told her that the blue shirts were behind
She said that she wished
They could all be blue shirts
Which would be interesting
A common time sheet shared by all

Monday, February 13, 2012

And so
It seems
Winter has finally rushed in
Wiping clear
Any memories
Of mildness

Brushing the very thought
Of temperate days away
Like sand and grit
Blown from the surface
Of an exposed
Time sheet

Monday, February 20, 2012

I got sick
Unexpectedly
Late on Saturday night
And spent the next day in bed
Partially awake
Partially asleep
Tangled in recurring dreams
That blended
Childcare and accounting

I kept dreaming
That the hours
I was not spending
With my children
Would need to be
Accounted for
Differently
At a reduced rate
But I wasn't able
To balance
The accounting

A hazy and addled
Time sheet
That I would find to be
Blank
Upon waking

Monday, February 27, 2012

We watched the trees
Swaying in the yard
Under heavy winds
But no damage was done
Some mid-sized branches
Fell by the fence
But nothing more
It was as though
The trees had simply woken up
To wave to us
In greeting
Reaching out
While we filled in
Our time sheets
From the comfort
Of indoors

Monday, March 5, 2012

I don't always know where my mind goes
But I know where it ends up
Inevitably during a renovation I find myself
Standing in the middle of the room late at night
At peace
So long as I've put in
The required number of hours for the day
Reviewing the work that has been done
Planning the moves of tomorrow
Trying to envision the final layout
Under a bare bulb awaiting its new fixture
A time sheet written over
With notes for purchases
And rough sketches of possible designs

Monday, March 12, 2012

Looking out the window
In the midst of prepping
Some shelves to be painted
I saw that all the neighbors
Who had been sequestered inside
For the winter
Were now out and about
Chatting at the ends
Of their fences

I myself
Was not yet ready
To emerge
As I had to choose
Between "Great Green"
And "Yarrow"

A tricky decision
Though a pleasant one
An old time sheet
Spackled
Planed
And primed
Ready to turn anew

Monday, March 19, 2012

I should have known that it was coming
But the spring caught me off guard
It seems as though all in an afternoon
The geese
Were suddenly returning overhead in batches
While the peepers called
In chorus from the ravine
And I found myself frantically
Pulling out the lawn furniture
Setting up tables and chairs
Filling the torches with oil
Throwing together a completely different
Kind of time sheet
All from elements that had been dormant
And somehow now were not

Monday, March 26, 2012

Nothing reminds me
More quickly
Of our connection
To the other animals
Than a sudden turn in the weather
Beyond the beetles and ants
Disoriented by the onset of blustery days
There is often
A palpable shift
Among people
Who struggle to drudge
Through muddled time sheets
That somehow don't seem
Quite right

Monday, April 2, 2012

A bird
Of some kind
Flew to the top of the tree
That's struggling to bloom
In our backyard
And chirped loudly
As I carried the bucket
Of vegetable trimmings
To the compost
This morning
A time sheet
Of annoyance and agitation

Monday, April 9, 2012

We buried coins in plastic eggs
For the second phase
Of the hunt
And worked with the children
To help sweep
The metal detector
Across the garden beds
Uncovering hidden
Quarters
And old garden hose stakes
In a flurry of beeping
And digging

Tiny shovels
Casting dirt
In all directions
Raining down on the time sheets
Unnoticed
At the edge
Of the garden bed

Monday, April 16, 2012

I have tremendous respect
For circus people

Constant travelling
With endless complex routines
That require perfect execution
And timing

Endlessly

I was awed by their performances
But still found my thoughts
Wandering
As I wondered
About their personal lives

How strange
Their time sheets
Must surely be

Monday, April 23, 2012

Most of the weeds
Grow simply
In the loose mulch
Gathering the wood chips
Together with their roots systems
But the violets
Pierce right through
The protective mesh
Underneath
And spread themselves wildly
Beholden to nothing
Erratic time sheets
Charging across
All projects

Monday, April 30, 2012

We fought the onslaught
Of a lingering cold spring
The best way possible
With giant artichokes
Steamed and drenched in butter

A time sheet
With the fancy top layers
Removed
Lest they be soaked
And stained
From melted wonderfulness

Monday, May 7, 2012

I'd be lying
If I said that it didn't take
An hour
To figure out how
To thread the sewing machine
Correctly

More than once
I experienced horrible jams
Between the bobbin
And the over-thread
In which I was certain
Something had happened
That was irreparable

But somehow
We sewed the jacket zipper
Onto the old
Decorative pillow
Extending its justification
For continuing to exist

A crafty and highly satisfying
Time sheet
Pinned
And sewn into place

Monday, May 14, 2012

We ended up with the robin eggs
As they had to be taken out of the eaves
Of a friend's house
Under construction
We had a week or so
Most likely
Before they hatched
So we ordered baby bird formula
And then went out locally
To get more when the order was delayed
We rotated the eggs
Under their lamp
In the makeshift nest
Of twigs and insulation
And candled them at night
To show the children
The flickering shadows of movement

But the odds
As we knew
Were against us

One by one
The shadows darkened
Though we left the lamp on
Long beyond the darkening of the last egg

Tonight we will place them
In the corner of the yard
By the tree where the creatures of years past
Have come to rest
Tiny blank time sheets
Prepped but unfulfilled

Monday, May 21, 2012

I don't know how
But I forgot the summer

I was surprised to hear
That it begins next weekend

I'd been too caught up
In the averageness of the spring

To see the muggy time sheets
Racing in from the distance

Tuesday, May 29, 2012

And so we return again
To the automation of the raised garden beds
Replacing the languid soaker hoses
Of previous years
With brusque impulse sprinkler heads

When the system activates
In the early morning
The rush of water
Through the jets
Sounds like thrusters
Fired on a rocket

Propelled clear across
From one time sheet to the next

Monday, June 4, 2012

We spent the day
Working with the others
Ratcheting together
Small sections
Of a community playground
In the heavy rain

I watched dust
Blow from the top
Of a giant pile of mulch
That was slowly being redistributed
With shovels and wheelbarrows
But a friend pointed out
That the mulch
Was in fact steaming

Individual pages
From the playground's manual
Lay all around
Soaked in loose plastic sleeves
Like sodden time sheets
Cast off by children at play

Monday, June 11, 2012

I'm getting to the point
That I must turn full circle
To acknowledge the things of the past
How they have or haven't changed

It is possible that
I won't finish
The periscope project
That seemed so close
A summer ago

It is possible that
The personality
Of the rabbit
Didn't change for the better
That he simply got old
And is less willing to run away

I'm not sure of the answers

I will simply submit
The week's time sheet
Without notes
In the comment field
And just watch for a while

Monday, June 18, 2012

At one point
While we sat on a bench
Waiting for the next heat
At the first annual
Musical Chairs World Championship
We spoke with some fellow contestants
Who happened to be cage fighters
And the young gentleman next to me
Showed us a necklace
Made from the tooth
Of a rival

His girlfriend excitedly stating
That the root
Went far deeper
Into the base of the charm
Than one would imagine

A strange and un-worldly time sheet
Filled with odd traces of the past

Friday, June 22, 2012 (For Monday)

Tonight I send you a note
In advance
As I shall be busy on Monday
Settled by a fire
At the base of mountains
I have no intention
Of climbing
Contemplating the nature
Of land
That was once passed back and forth
In battle
Between the British
And the French
Though its time sheets
Have long since settled
Coming to rest
As northern New England

Monday, July 2, 2012

We were delayed in moving
The butterfly chrysalises
From their original jar
As we'd been travelling
When they transformed

The morning after we returned
I pinned the thin paper
Where they resided
To the side of their mesh cage
And moved to step away
When one of them began to wiggle

We found out later
It was not on the verge
Of emerging
But rather
Was warding off the predator
It perceived me to be
A wonderful adaptation
I would never have guessed existed
Strange entries
On metamorphic time sheets

Monday, July 9, 2012

Perhaps it was a silly thing
That shouldn't have been done
But I pulled
All the wayward upstairs doors
Off their hinges
And sanded and planed them
For hours
Until they closed
And now
For the first time
In years
They close and latch
And I can't tell you
The satisfaction
Woven into this
The tiniest of time sheet events

Monday, July 16, 2012

We spent Saturday dabbling
On the shores of Lake Kingston
Exploring the depths
That stretched out
From the docks
At the base of the pavilion
That bustled on the hill
Above us

We hunted through the sands
For freshwater mussels
Treasures to be held aloft
And shown to others as remarkable proof
Of a moment in time
A snapshot on a time sheet
The record
Of a perfect summer day

Monday, July 23, 2012

I don't know why
But the dragonflies
Are enormous this year
Patrolling the backyard
Landing and lifting off
Like phosphorescent helicopter gunships
Calmly filling their time sheets
With details of the hunt

Sunday, July 29, 2012

Tonight we rode bikes
Out to dinner
With the children
And scribbled with crayons
While the meals were prepared
Tomorrow we will decide
Between petting zoos and amusement parks
And the time sheets
May wait
For another day

Monday, August 6, 2012

I take my hat off
To the fruit fly

Invisible to me
Until it swarms up
From the counter
To reclaim
A particular piece of fruit

I perceive
Perhaps erroneously
In the frantic bumbling
Of its movements
A sense of its own
Rapidly burning
Time sheet

An accounting of time
That is going not up
But down

Monday, August 13, 2012

My father had seen a sign
On the highway
For a band
He'd been interested in
Forty years ago
So we went to see them
At a club on the beach

We chatted amiably at our table
Waiting for the music to start
And I couldn't tell
If he fell asleep briefly
During the opening act

But when the headliner came on
He sat up
Took out his hearing aid
And jammed pieces of napkin
Into his ears
Before sitting back with a smile

Able to close out
An old pending project
Dating back countless time sheets
Something ancient and very far away

Monday, August 20, 2012

Straightening up the backyard
As dusk approached
After the party
I was surprised to hear the geese call overhead
And thought
"There must be some mistake"
It seemed too soon

They were moving too quickly
And I was able to follow them
For only a moment
Twenty strong
No languorous V formations
But rather a single straight line
Just above the tops of the trees

The next morning
There was talk of breaking down
The inflatable pool for the season
And I had not seen any of this coming
The premature end of the season
Irrevocable irreversible
Time sheets already entered and submitted
Charges billed out
Projects and clients closed
Marked as completed
Over and
Done

Monday, August 27, 2012

Tonight we will meet the person
From the performing arts troupe
Who will be staying with us
For the week
A man
Or a woman
From one of the nations
Equipped
We are told
With conversational English
And a pair of free tickets
To the show

It is to be a week
Of unpredictable
Time sheet entries

Tuesday, September 4, 2012

Of course
The summer isn't really over at all
It will go on, as it does
For several more weeks
But it is hard to acknowledge sometimes
That a significant part
Of the season
Is in fact cooler and mild

Tinged with melancholy
As much as the deepest autumn

So be it
We will handle it
As we may
Writing in "fall" on our time sheets
A little earlier than we should
Then go about our way

Monday, September 10, 2012

This is the weather for me
Dappled sun
With long shadows

Bracing currents of air
Not cold
But not warm either

A time sheet alive
With the motion of the plants
And the insects
Along the edges of the pavement

Friday, September 14, 2012 (For Monday)

There is always more to it
Whatever it is
The sadness of the above ground pool
Being taken down
Is quickly dissipated
By the surprise re-emergence
Of the dirt hole beneath it
A fabled eight-foot circle of earth
Cleared of all debris and roughly level
Flattened by the seasonal presence of the pool

The dirt calls to the children
As much, if not more, than the water
And before it is even finished draining
We are rolling up the sodden edges
To pluck the grubs out from their sleep
A time sheet frantically dug out
With trowels and spades
Cascading showers of earth
In all directions

Monday, September 24, 2012

On the first day
Of the season
We found ourselves
Putting away the lighter bedspreads
And pulling out the stout ones
Shuttling bins of seasonal clothes
Up and down the stairs
And returning the air conditioners
To their darkened perches
In the basement
Time sheets of order and preparation
Pulled forward
By the season itself

Monday, October 1, 2012

I couldn't find the switch
To the bathroom
So I went in
In the dark
With a small light emitting diode
On my hat
To illuminate the way

A moth flew under the stall door
And landed on the tile
Near to me
Its body appeared in the light
As I expected
But its eye
Was an orange burning ember
Straight from the coals of the fire

The moth flew away
Then returned again

And I looked for it when I left
Hoping to ferry it outside
On a piece of paper or a leaf
But it was gone

Returned, perhaps, as I was
To the fire outside
To the telling of time sheets
Old half-forgotten stories
Of long ago
And far away

Monday, October 8, 2012

Rounding the cobblestone flower circle
At the edge of the yard
On the final mowing of the season
I looked up to see
Dead standing sunflowers
Rising above the wild grasses

The plants were thin and taut and brittle
With no remnants of green
But the flower heads brown and bare
Still stood
Pointed to the air
Far above me
Taller in death than I in life
A still time sheet
An ancient tableau
Caught and held by unseen forces

Monday, October 15, 2012

We went to a tree farm
To tag a tree
For harvesting
This winter
And chose a blue spruce
Not far from the road

Affixing the tag given us
To the upper branches
Didn't seem enough
To cement the tree's place
In our future
So we rummaged around in the car

And came up with a small rubber duck
And a plastic hand-clapper toy
That we tied up
With some frayed string
To dangle above us
Until our return

Estimated projections
On a seasonal time sheet
That has yet to occur

Monday, October 22, 2012

Walking from the car
Across a grass parking lot
At the edge of the apple orchard
We passed under enormous maple trees
Impossibly brilliant and light
Orange and yellow time sheets
Rustling above us
While we sloshed through the fallen below

Monday, October 29, 2012

I went out in the morning dark
To feed the rabbit
And stood below the giant trees
Which seemed to me
In the growing winds
To be talking to one another
About what's to come
Project managers forecasting
The time sheets ahead

Monday, November 5, 2012

I pulled the broken snow thrower
Into the backyard
In the late morning
And worked on it
To be prepared
For an unknown winter

The day moved on
And I had a vague sense
Of the sun moving across the lawn
Then it was beyond the fence
Until I'd lost decent light altogether

It was in the gray before the real darkness
With cold hands and sore legs
That I broke a critical piece
On the recoil-starter
And lost a screw
For good measure

Forced to wheel what was left
Back to the garage
With gasoline hands
And a worn spirit
I barely had the resolve
To order the new part
On the computer

A loss of time and focus
Foolish misguided time sheet entries
More painful than banged fingers

Monday, November 12, 2012

A fabulous international party
On Saturday night
Was followed by treasure hunting
On the beach
With my parents and the girls
On Sunday morning
Ending in a fantastic lobster lunch

It was a wonderful weekend
Without question
Time sheets filled with miraculous things

But I am a prince of simple things
And Monday perhaps
Trumped it all
Successfully installing
The replacement recoil-starter
On the old snow thrower
And having it roar to life
As though new
Affirmed in a second
All the lost wasted hours
That had been spent before
In pursuit of that very thing

Monday, November 19, 2012

Watching a movie
With our older cat asleep
Under the covers
A baby began to cry
On the television
And the cat shot out
From under the comforter
To stand frozen
On the bed
Fully alert
Pointing to the girls' room
Until the cry of the television
Quieted down

It made me think
About the perspectives
Of our animals
The concerns that they carry

The cat perhaps did not know
The girls are no longer babies
And that they rarely cry out
In the night
Anymore

Or perhaps
She knew this
But was startled awake
And returned to maternal instincts
I did not know that she possessed
Strange time sheet entries in the night
The inner workings of which
I shall never see

Monday, November 26, 2012

I went to my 20th high school reunion
Reluctantly with a friend
I'd studied the names and faces beforehand
But found I had little context
For most of the people

The conversations were pleasant
But short
Spouses, houses, children and employment
Then awkward silences

I found it best to step away
At those points
Better to stand alone at a table
Than try to struggle through

My friend remarked that next to our names
We should have written what elementary schools
We attended
And he was right
As I found that I gravitated most
To the kids I'd walked to school with long ago
Vague and casual acquaintances
Many of whom I'd lost sight of
By the time high school had started

It was like trying to peer back
To read forward-looking time sheet entries
Written in a child's scrawl
All but indecipherable now

Monday, December 3, 2012

I arrived a few minutes early
As Santa Claus
At the request of the Newburyport mother's club
An organization of eight hundred moms
That had been unable to find
Another volunteer

Some children and their parents
Had arrived even earlier than I
And so I was whisked away
To a storage room
In the back

The organizer searched briefly
For the light
Then apologized
And closed the door quickly
Behind her
But I did not mind

I stood in the darkness
With the other items
And we listened
To the excitement
Of the children
As the final underpinnings of the party
Were put into place

The time sheets prepped
The stage set
An old actor
Waiting quietly
In the wings

Monday, December 10, 2012

My oldest daughter's front tooth
Had been wiggly for some time
We'd been watching it
And talking about it
As it was her first

So we were all surprised
To discover on Friday night
That it was simply gone

She had no recollection of losing it
And a quick search of the house
Turned up nothing

My wife later announced
Matter-of-factly
That she had eaten it
Which luckily unsettled her less than I

Regardless the tooth fairy would still come
Leaving a golden coin
That somehow impossibly
Is still only worth a dollar

This final detail
I am perhaps more loath
To have to explain
Than all of the mystical workings behind it

Our time sheets swirling
With a wild blend of the mystical
And the ordinary

Monday, December 17, 2012

I brought the rabbit in last night
During the storm
Huddled against my stomach
Like a package that had been forgotten
And then hastily retrieved from the snow

I don't know how old he is
He was six or seven
When we got him
Six or seven years ago

He will winter
In the basement hutch
And if he's up for it
We will return him outside
In the early spring

A small and furry notation
On our time sheets
Marking the passage forward

Wednesday, December 26, 2012

We made red velvet cupcakes last night
Each no larger than an inch

Cooked to perfection
In a purple plastic oven

I added too much water
To the frosting
As I am not known
For my cooking

But I was graciously forgiven
And we quickly moved on
To plastic blocks
And lighted pegs
Rummaging through the gifts
Of the day
Wonderfully assembled time sheets
Built, cooked, stickered, and stacked together

Monday, December 31, 2012

We made snowmen
On the back porch

Prior to the arrival
Of the storm

With the leftover dustings
From earlier in the week

Sad little conical snow people
Hard pressed
And brittle
Slumping down onto the deck

Creatures born
To inopportune time sheets
Between storms

Monday, January 7, 2013

I removed the outdoor lights
Without incident
As the day was warm and pleasant

It was the extension cord
Deeply frozen
Into a block of ice
That I did not have
The strength or the patience for

The wire was taught and immobile
Beneath the clear and transparent ice

A time sheet's annotation
This winter is just beginning

Stephen R Wagner

Monday, January 21, 2013

My daughter called me into her room
On Sunday morning
To watch the giant pine tree behind our house
Interacting with the wind

"The tree's dancing,"
She said

A statement made
Without qualification
No metaphors or similes
Needed

As she could see the nature of things
For herself
Her time sheet
Unclouded

Monday, February 4, 2013

We have reached
In our home
An era of high construction
Where most loose materials
Are subject to be cut up
Into pieces
Then glued taped and stapled
Back together

The tape dispensers
Have been released
To the children
And whenever I reach for one
I find that it has
In fact
Been used up
Entirely

The white roll in the center
Glistens like a bone
From a fallen animal
Laid to waste
In the sun
On a time sheet
From long ago

Monday, February 11, 2013

As I was struggling
To get the snowblower
Through several feet of snow
My six-year-old daughter
Came outside
With a large domed umbrella
In the shape of a ladybug

She made her way
To the center of the yard
And then sat down
Disappearing
Into the snow

She remained there
For quite some time
Under her lowered umbrella
Enjoying
I imagine
The strange diffuse light
Of the dome
Cast on the snowiest time sheet
She had ever seen

Monday, February 18, 2013

There is a Grand Cherokee
At the end of the parking lot
That has lost its grandness
Abandoned
Halfway in
And halfway out
Of a parking spot

A front tire sunken
Resting on its rim
Deflated

Left for days

The snow and wind
Batter on about
And there is an eeriness to it

A time sheet
Abruptly at an end

Monday, February 25, 2013

I watched parts of an amazing series
On crows
During brief breaks
From the renovation
Of my mudroom

I learned how crows
Gather wire clothes hangers
And shape them
To fit their bodies
As part of their nests

And it occurred to me
As I measured and cut boards
Down to within a sixteenth of an inch
That this was in fact what I was doing

A time sheet fully occupied
Shaping the parameters
Of my nest
To fit the bodies that live therein

Monday, March 4, 2013

Carrying an empty can
To the recycling bin
I turned it over in my hand
And found a ladybug
Crawling across the lip

I spent five minutes outside
By the dirt alongside the driveway
Trying to coax it off
But couldn't

It was too cold anyway
So I brought it back inside
And we settled on a plant by the sink
A quiet time sheet in the winter night
The harbinger of spring

Monday, March 11, 2013

Three houses
A town away from where I live
Fell into the ocean
And twelve more
Are no longer capable
Of sustaining life

The oceans are coming

The only thing that's not certain
Is the specific timeline
And what to tell the children

A time sheet of conversations
About the weather
That keeps ending in soft murmurs
On the reflection
That it has been getting worse

Monday, March 18, 2013

The rabbit is getting old
There is no question of this
But he is still kicking

It is time to bring him out
From the basement
To his hutch outside

It is still cold
But he is still a rabbit

Perhaps
I think
While I am cleaning the hutch
I will bring him out
During the storm
So that he may watch it
From the yard

A remarkable time sheet of spectacle and flurry
A good way to end out the winter
To knock away the basement doldrums

Sunday, March 24, 2013 (For Monday)

I dug a large container of rotten greens
And the morning's coffee grounds
Out of the kitchen trash
To put them in the seasonal bucket
That we use for compost
To carry the seeds and the cores and the rinds
To the piles behind the shed

We store the bucket away
In our winter
When the snow makes the frequent journeys
No longer worthwhile

There was a brief discussion
When I first went to retrieve it
From its resting place in the basement

Is it worth it?
Should we even bother?

I had little doubt that it was and we should
A small but life affirming gesture
On an infinitely-wide time sheet
Spreading out before us

Monday, April 1, 2013

I was clearing dead branches
In the small space
Between the back of the shed
And the fence
When three geese
Flew over
So low
So close
And so fast and so loud
That they seemed like
Jet fighters
Heralding the spring
Envoys of hope and motion
Calling down
A time sheet of rejuvenation
Curling green beneath my feet

Monday, April 8, 2013

There is an old photo
On my mother's bureau
Of my grandfather
At the beach
Wearing a dark black coat
Slightly bent over
Poking at the sand
With his walking stick

My brother and I
Are digging around his feet
As very small children

I thought of this
As I crested a small hill
On one of the nightly stout walks
I now take with my two little girls

It is now I who has a walking stick
From England in fact
With a compass
And a small hidden vial
For refreshment

Slightly bent over in my dark black coat
I poke at the baby pinecones
And other treasures
That we find and discuss
As we amble along
The edge of the road

Time sheets of small and miraculous discoveries

Monday, April 15, 2013

I took my motorcycle
Off the charger
Designed to keep it vital
In its dormancy
And rolled it
Into the light of the day
Onto a time sheet
Of unknown prospects

Unclear if it or I
Were ready

But we were
And it was tremendous

It is hard to describe
But it is like
Being buoyed up
By twenty people
At your door
With tools and nourishment
Fanning out around you
Pruning and painting
Watering and weeding
Cultivating and tending
The very soil
On which you are standing

That is what it is like
And it is a good thing

Monday, April 22, 2013

The cat got sick
Shortly after I did
She got thin
And started spending all her time
Curled up on my lap

We took her to the vet and got her tested
They ruled out everything but cancer
So that's what it was

There's not much you can do with a cat
At that point
They don't understand
Chemotherapies and surgeries
So you curl up with them
And enjoy their company

She was watching me from the end of the bed
So I said, "I'll make a deal with you."
"I'll try to live, if you try to live."
And you know
Right that very second
She meowed very loudly
And it almost sounded like
"I will."
So I picked her up
And sat with her
And we had a great afternoon
I am worried I am becoming spoiled
Even the pets are reaching out to help me
A time sheet that fits
Comfortably over my shoulders
Like a cloak

Monday, April 29, 2013

The rabbit died peacefully
In the night

I wore gloves
When I carried it down
To the bottom of the ravine
With the shovel
Because the metal
Makes my fingers tingle

I let the rabbit down gently
By a tree
Along the edge of the creek
An offering to the creatures
That run in the night
Beneath the edges
Of the time sheets

Monday, May 6, 2013

I dug the pit for the fish pond
Over the weekend
Sitting beneath a beach umbrella
Resting intermittently
When the heartburn
From the medicine kicked in
And tonight I will level the preformed liner
On a thin bed of sand
Then add the water

Tomorrow morning
The solar pump will kick on
Circulating the water
Through diverters and sprayers
And the pond plants
Though all somewhat wilted
From having waited in a bucket
The pond plants will swirl
At the surface

And then we shall add the fish
Small feeder-goldfish
The often sickly and devoured
Slaves of the fish world

We shall empower our feeder fish
To school at their own will
If they choose to
Taking their own chances
Living in the open air
And among the rocks
In a swarm of orange opalescence
On a time sheet of their own making

Monday, May 13, 2013

It felt good to work my hands in the earth
My nails scratched and foggy
With the cuticles pushed back
Digging out around the perimeter
Of the fish pond
Adding some edging and some stones

After everything was set
I went to the store
And bought three dollar's worth of fish

Twenty-four feeder fish in total
I still can't believe
They have so little value

After the temperature
Of their bag
Reached the temperature
Of the pond
I cut off the top
And released them
And they instantly disappeared
Into the murky brown water
Clouded by the mud and clay
From the river stones

But I look for them each day

And as the water slowly clears
Glimpses of them emerge
Orange blurs
Moving in the darkness at the bottom
On a time sheet that is becoming clearer

Tuesday, May 21, 2013

It is reassuring to see
The feeder fish
Hit at the surface of the water
At the flakes above them
In the early light
As the dogwood cherry blossoms
Continue to drift down past the swing set

There are signs of new ant holes
And spots where the skunks
Have dug in the night for grubs

All is proceeding
As it should
Though I am a day behind
In the tracking of time
And the officiating of time sheets
The backyard it seems
Shall forgive me

Tuesday, May 28, 2013

In order to thoroughly clean
The dining room table
I had to address the large vase filled with flowers
I had given to my wife several weeks ago

The roses had wilted
And the green filler sprigs were rotten
I thought about pitching
The whole thing
Into the compost bin

But the tiger lilies
Were still doing remarkably well
And the Gerber daisies
Stood proud and bright
Along with some other flowers
I could not name

So I mucked out the vase
Picked through the detritus
Culled the waste
And filled it with fresh water

When I was done
It looked so good
It practically radiated its own light

I was glad I had seen it through
For these are times of arduous pruning
Necessary to sustain and maintain the whole

A time sheet of preservation and rejuvenation

Monday, June 3, 2013

I took my oldest daughter
To our first father-daughter dance
And we had a nice time milling around

I had gotten her a wrist corsage
With a yellow rose
To match her bright dress
But perhaps I ordered it too soon
Or they just don't keep well
As the petals browned
And fell off at the dance

But the next day
We glued an overly large plastic flower
Onto the corsage band
In place of the lost rose
And we are both rather taken with it

It will last
Even though it isn't real

A moment on a time sheet
Captured in plastic
And I don't know why
But it makes me smile so
To see it

Monday, June 10, 2013

The grass is coming in well
The inflatable pool is full
The solar post lights
Come on dutifully at dusk
And the various trees
Around the house
Take turns blooming
As the goldfish nip
At the surface of the fish pond

All systems are go
For the summer
A time sheet of preparedness
And joy
That unfolds like a flower
In the morning sun

Monday, June 17, 2013

We finally had to put the cat down
Her muscles had wasted away
And she couldn't keep her paws or her face clean
Then her kidneys went
And it was time

It was tricky for me to reconcile
That our paths had to diverge
That I couldn't see her through her cancer
Even though it was inevitable

She had had a good run
A long and unbroken time sheet
That wove through our lives like a tapestry
From the moment I picked her up
At the rescue shelter as a kitten
To the moment I laid her back down
Seven years later
Onto the small blanket
On the veterinarian's table
After she'd been given
The preliminary anesthesia
Just prior
To the final fatal dose

Saturday, June 22, 2013 (For Monday)

I will not be sending you a poem
On Monday
As I shall be at the beach on vacation
Very busy with important things
Like creating treasure maps
And burying golden-dollar coins
Watching the children
Sweep the beach
With the metal detector
A time sheet of ancient and new treasures
Buried just below the surface

Monday, July 1, 2013

We spent the days
At the various beaches
Shopping and exploring a little
With the children

On Thursday night though
My wife and I went out
To dinner and a show
And then I took her to Purgatory
Where we were the only ones
Who were dancing

A time sheet in a darkened subterranean club
Illuminated only
By the disco balls and light machines
Spinning around us

Monday, July 29, 2013

My hair has thinned
Much quicker than I expected
It's still there
But I can easily see through to my scalp

I've thought of shaving it off
Or cutting it very short
But at the same time
I want to watch it
And see what it does

And then figure out
How to rise above it

A time sheet firmly rooted
In expectations and imaginings
Of future time sheets
That have yet to clearly occur

Monday, August 5, 2013

Convalescence is a strange creature
Previously unknown to me

It is only now
A month out
As the taste of food returns
And the distance I may walk increases
While discomforts begin to recede
Into the background
That I may see the entire process with clarity
And finally feel the kernels of strength
That grow mildly stronger each day

Now that I and my wounds
Have finished weeping
I may look to the radiation
And the chemotherapies and the surgeries
On the time sheets ahead
With assurance and determination

And I welcome them

Monday, August 12, 2013

We arrived
At the river
In the mid-afternoon

They lowered our canoe into the water
And we paddled upstream
Stopping along a shallow ledge
To allow the children
To bob and wade
In their vests

On the way back
We grabbed some cattails
From the shore
And the girls pulled out the seeds
In small tufts
Casting them to the water
As I guided our canoe back downstream
Through the dappled light
Of the late afternoon

A time sheet of water bugs
Lily pads
And long underwater grasses
That seemed to wave up to us
As we passed

Monday, August 19, 2013

It is good to get out
To shake off the dust
To break up the quiet hours of reading
In the corner bedroom
Where the lamp always seems to be on

We went to a jazz fest
By the ocean
To see some old college friends perform

We blew bubbles and ate ice cream
And the children rolled down the grassy slopes
In ecstasy
A late summer afternoon time sheet
Surrounded by the harbor
And the boats that reach beyond

Monday, August 26, 2013

As I was finishing the dishes
Late Sunday night
Listening to one of my albums
It occurred to me
That I had abandoned music
At my lowest point

I had pushed it away
For a month after my surgery
To protect it
As I'd become adverse
To various tastes and odors
At my worst
And had been wary of further aversions

But in the kitchen
The music roared back
Loud and alive
As I scrubbed down the counters

And I could tell
That I myself
Was starting to come back
Travelling along the edge
Of a thriving time sheet
Readying to cross back
Into the thick of it

Stephen R Wagner

Tuesday, September 3, 2013

There is a tree
On my street
On which the leaves have already begun
To turn and fall
But when I lay in bed at night
If I listen for it
I can still hear the crickets chirping
A time sheet
Summery enough
For now

Monday, September 9, 2013

When I curl up with my little one
To put her to bed
And she insists
On rubbing my back
It is hard to not get a little teary
And it occurs to me
It would be a crime
To not survive for this little girl
So that is exactly what I'll do
A small and friendly time sheet
Of warmth and encouragement

Monday, September 16, 2013

As we were driving home from shopping
An acorn fell through my open window
And landed on my hand
The children examined it
And when we got home
We planted it in a long-vacant pot
That had been standing by the window
Which was waiting
I guess
For this acorn

I don't know if anything will come of it
But I like to think it will grow

A time sheet spent ruminating
On advancements in the seed dispersal systems
Of plants

Monday, September 23, 2013

After touring artists' fairy houses
We settled down in Prescott Park
To make our own
With the materials provided

We leaned sticks and twigs together
With flowers and leaves
And scattered dried out lobster tails
Around the bases

Forming patios with sea shells
And large green leaves
We created fantastical houses
For fantastical creatures
A constructive time sheet
In the wind and sun

The true start of fall

Monday, September 30, 2013

Late at night
When the campfire roared
To its largest size
The trees were still and dark
But the lowest branches
Far above us
Swayed and danced

Animated by the air currents
As were the people
Gathered around
A garrulous time sheet
Of laughter and exclamations

Monday, October 7, 2013

They surprised me
With a party
I hadn't seen coming

Perhaps a hundred people
Or more
Dancing and laughing
Into the night
With children running
In all directions

A retrospective time sheet
Of tremendous warmth and kindness
I am indebted to them all

Monday, October 14, 2013

I put two dozen feeder fish
Into our preformed fish pond
At the beginning
Of the summer
And then quickly lost track of them
Distracted
With one thing or another
Until the surface of the water disappeared
Beneath the leaves of the water lilies
And it was no longer clear
What lurked beneath

When the summer ended
We discovered
That some golden fish survived
So we dredged the pond
Netted them
And brought them inside
To shepherd them through the winter
A time sheet of renewed and invigorated efforts
To see them through the coming storms

Monday, October 21, 2013

We placed the goldfish
From the abandoned fish pond
Into our Oscar's tank
And put a divider between them

But the goldfish are small
And swim freely
Past the barrier
Designed to save them

We panicked at first
And struggled to separate them
But the Oscar is old and lethargic
And pays them no mind

The goldfish seem oblivious
They swarm and shimmer and shine
Churning in the corners

A time sheet of twisting abandon

But they are smarter than they seem
And return to their side
Each night
As it grows dark
Remaining there until the light

Monday, November 4, 2013

I spent much of the weekend
Tidying the basement
Sweeping and organizing
Sorting through ancient piles
Dragging up bins of old toys
That the children feverishly picked through
Claiming the best forgotten prizes
The rest destined for community yard sales
Recycling and the trash

I had to push against the urge
To save everything
That could be put to some use
It was best to remind myself
That most pieces
Regardless of how promising
Would not serve a higher function
So be it

I had to throw away dozens
Of sealed little baggies
From my workbench
Cheap prepackaged nails and screws
That come with so many things
Crummy thin screws
With easily stripped threads
I had saved them
Thinking that perhaps
They'd be perfect for some foolish project
But they would not
A time sheet of reason and logic
Breaking the stringy sticky ties
To the leftover pieces of things

Monday, November 11, 2013

Having fully recovered from my first surgery
As my second surgery approaches
I have been thinking
About what constitutes
The return to my old self
I now feel I have achieved

It is made up of many parts certainly
Working and getting chores done
Spending time with family and friends
But there is more
It is a return to the mending of things
That helps make me whole
A complicated clamping and gluing
Of a cardboard doll house's
Warped paper floors
Or the simple bending
Of a metal contact
Inside a child's flashlight
To restore the shining of the light
This is what
I shall look to do
As I recover from my second and possibly final surgery
I shall hope
For a rapid repair
Of my own body
So that I may return
To the fixing of wayward things

A time sheet spent
Infusing purpose and life
To the broken and passed by

Monday, November 18, 2013

Tomorrow morning
In the early hours
Before my procedure
I shall play my ukulele

A gift given to me
A month ago
For my birthday

I have not missed a day
Of practice
Since I received it
And I have no intention
Of starting now

A musical time sheet
With an emphasis
On perfecting
The transition

Moving
From one chord
To the next
Beyond

Monday, November 25, 2013

I watched the tops
Of the bare trees
I could see from my window
Today

As the sun passed down
Through them
Glaring up
Brighter and brighter
And then dimming

I drifted
In and out of sleep
Content
With the medication
And the warmth of my bed

A time sheet spent
In and out of time

Tuesday, December 3, 2013

I went on my daily walk
In the late afternoon
As the blue of the upper sky
Was darkening to black

I carried a small flashlight
That glowed green
A wand just bright enough
To illuminate the outline
Of the sidewalk before me

At the edge of the woods
Where the sidewalk ends
A speck of something
Caught my eye
And I stopped

Tiny white moths
Exploded into the night
Appearing and disappearing
Flying off rakishly into nothing
Like sparks

As though the very edges
Of a time sheet
Had broken off
And burst into flight

Monday, December 9, 2013

As a passenger
During the storm
I watched the trees
Flash by
Along the edge of the road

The tops of the branches
White with wet snow
The bottoms of the branches
Brown and bare
Frozen arms
Pointing upwards
To the sky

A time sheet
Of slush
Kicking up
On the highway

On my way
To get the stitches out

Monday, December 16, 2013

My fish died over the weekend
But it didn't go as I'd imagined
There was no surprise or suspense
It was more than ten years old
And it had stopped eating
A month before
It simply gave up
And sat on the bottom of the tank
Breathing rhythmically
Watching me
Until it didn't anymore

If it had shown any inkling
Of trying to eat
I could have worked with it
I could have continued to hand-feed it
Holding the slippery superworms
In place
With a plastic grabber
As I had done for the last few years
But it made its choice
And never waivered
I was angry because it wasn't even sad
In the end I was simply tired
I had to lay it to rest
On the compost pile
Because the ground was too cold
Too frozen
For me to break through
A time sheet to mark the end of an era
The passing of the last of the great fish
Fully a quarter as old as I

Monday, December 23, 2013

Today I cleaned the fish tank
For the first time
Since the last of the big fish died

I removed the heavy plastic divider
That had been separating it
Into two
And spruced things up a bit

I was impressed
As I worked
That all thirteen
Of the goldfish
Rescued from the pond
Were still alive

They are babies
These goldfish
And I have heard
That they can live
For twenty years

And so
We begin again

A time sheet of camaraderie

We are the survivors
The goldfish and I

Monday, December 30, 2013

With all the tensions of the year
I experimented for a while
With shouting
To see if it would help
But it didn't

And so
As the year ends
I am leaving shouting behind

I've been working more closely
With the children
Getting back in touch with them
And you should hear
The songs we've been singing

A time sheet of beautiful sounds
Rising up and down
Held in time
For just a few notes

Monday, January 6, 2014

And so
I am cancer free
For now
What more
Could anyone ask for?

It is not clear
What the future holds
But that
Is the very beautiful essence
Of the future

I wouldn't have it any other way

I step forward
Achy and sore
With some parts missing

Time now to fill out
A literal time sheet
A few hours a day at first
Building up
Charging slowly
Gathering momentum
Readying to burst through the roof
To see the faraway stars

About the Author

Stephen lives. He continues to work and try, even though it often ends in failure. He believes it's worth it, even when it isn't. And for all the writing and learning to play an instrument, he still hasn't learned how to draw.

62638362R00151

Made in the USA
Middletown, DE
25 January 2018